Right-Now Faith

David M. Blunt

RIGHT-NOW FAITH
by David M. Blunt
ISBN 1-893716-07-4

Table of Contents

Dedication

To my wife, Kim,
and my two sons, Daniel and Stephen.
To God be the glory!

INTRODUCTION

A Right-Now God

Immediately. That's the deadline most of us prefer when we want something. NOW. Not tomorrow. Not next week. Not next month. Not five years down the road. Right now.

In fact, our society has become so accustomed to right-now living that most people wouldn't know how to function any other way. Instant coffee. Instant tea. Instant information. Fast food. Fast cash. Fast cars. And, boy, if it's not there when we want it, somebody's going to pay!

But when it comes to receiving from God, many people do a complete turnaround. When it comes to God, they live in the Someday Zone. "Maybe *someday* God will save me." "Maybe *someday* God will heal me." "Maybe *someday* God will deliver me." "Maybe *someday* God will bless me." Everything is always going to happen *someday*.

Don't get me wrong. I'm not saying that we need to start snapping our fingers and expecting God to jump. But the truth is that if we stay in the Someday Zone, we'll never receive all that He has for us. In order to receive from God, we have to move into the realm of the now.

If you're one of those people who have been living in the Someday Zone, I've got good news for you. God is *not* a someday God. He's a right-now God. He cares about you right now and He wants to bless you right now. You don't have to wait until someday. He's ready and willing to work in your life today. Right now. Immediately.

If you're content to put off the blessings of God until someday, then this isn't the book for you. But if you want to see God manifest Himself in your circumstances right now, then keep reading. By the time you're through, I believe you'll know how to exercise the kind of faith that gets immediate results.

Pastor David M. Blunt

Chapter 1

The Story Of Blind Bartimaeus

Blind. Begging. Sitting on the side of the road. That's Bartimaeus when we first meet him in the Bible. Not a very pretty picture. But there's more to his story. Much more.

In Mark 10, we find the story of the man whom the Scriptures identify as "blind Bartimaeus."

> Mark 10:46–52
>
> 46 *And they came to Jericho: and as he went out of Jericho with his disciples and a great number of people, blind Bartimaeus, the son of Timaeus, sat by the highway side begging.*
>
> 47 *And when he heard that it was Jesus of Nazareth, he began to cry out, and say, Jesus, thou son of David, have mercy on me.*
>
> 48 *And many charged him that he should hold his peace: but he cried the more a great deal, Thou son of David, have mercy on me.*
>
> 49 *And Jesus stood still, and commanded him to be called. And they call the blind man, saying*

unto him, Be of good comfort, rise; he calleth thee.

50 *And he, casting away his garment, rose, and came to Jesus.*

51 *And Jesus answered and said unto him, What wilt thou that I should do unto thee? The blind man said unto him, Lord, that I might receive my sight.*

52 *And Jesus said unto him, Go thy way; thy faith hath made thee whole. And immediately he received his sight, and followed Jesus in the way.*

Although we first see Bartimaeus as a blind beggar, sitting on the side of the road, we can also see that he wasn't satisfied with that kind of life. He wanted something more. He wanted to live the life God created him to live. And when Jesus came his way, Bartimaeus knew that was his chance.

Bartimaeus wanted something from God–and he got it. And not only did he get it, but he got it immediately. Now that's a testimony worth studying!

We're going to go back and look at this story again, verse by verse. But first, let's envision the setting. Jesus and His disciples are on their way from Jericho to Jerusalem to observe Passover. Jesus' popularity is riding high. There's a great crowd of people traveling with Him. Soon He's going to be making His triumphal entry into the city of Jerusalem amidst the shouts and praises of the multitudes.

In spite of all this, Jesus knows that His time of ministering here on earth is drawing to a close. Very soon, He will be agonizing in prayer in the Garden of Gethsemane, then led away to be tortured and eventually crucified for the sins of the whole world. He has probably never been more focused than He is at this point in His life. He's a Man on a mission. He's a Man with a purpose. He knows He has a mandate from God. He's going somewhere.

But suddenly, Jesus stops in His tracks. What was so important? What arrested His attention? Why did He stop? To respond to the faith of Bartimaeus. And that encounter with Jesus changed the life of Bartimaeus forever.

That's the story in a nutshell, but now let's go over some of the details a little more closely. After all, Bartimaeus exercised the kind of faith that got the attention of God and brought immediate results. I believe we can learn a few things from his example.

Verse 46

> *And they came to Jericho: and as he went out of Jericho with his disciples and a great number of people, blind Bartimaeus, the son of Timaeus, sat by the highway side begging.*

As the story begins, Bartimaeus isn't much of a player. He's on the side of the road, out of the action. But he definitely knew how to pick his spots. Jericho was a large, wealthy city about 15 miles away from Jerusalem. It was located on a very busy, well-traveled route. If you were a beggar, it was a good place to be.

Verse 47

> *And when he heard that it was Jesus of Nazareth, he began to cry out, and say, Jesus, thou son of David have mercy on me.*

Verse 47 tells us that when Bartimaeus heard that Jesus was passing by, he cried out to Him, "Jesus, thou son of David, have mercy on me." That's significant because it tells us something very important about Bartimaeus. It tells us that he was a believer.

How do we know that? "Son of David" is a messianic term. Although the Pharisees sometimes used it to mock Jesus, the term was primarily used by people who recognized Him as the Messiah. Bartimaeus was one of those people.

Blind. Begging. But a believer. How did that happen? How did Bartimaeus come to be a believer? By hearing the Word of God.

Romans 10:17 says that faith comes ". . . by hearing, and hearing by the word of God." Faith comes by hearing the Word of God. So if Bartimaeus was a believer, it must have been because he had heard the prophecies from the Word of God about the Messiah. He must have heard that the Messiah was going to make the blind see. He must have heard that the Messiah was going to make the lame walk. He must have heard that the Messiah was going to make the deaf hear. He must have heard that the Messiah was going to preach good news to the poor. And he must have also heard that this Jesus of Nazareth was doing all of those miraculous things everywhere He went. He must have heard.

Faith comes by hearing the Word of God.

But he also must have seen. He must have seen that Jesus was the fulfillment of those prophecies. He must have seen that the Messiah, the Anointed One, the Promised One had finally come and was right there, living among them. He must have seen that his situation wasn't hopeless anymore now that God was in the picture. He must have seen.

Funny, isn't it? A blind man was able to recognize the presence of God when others around him didn't. The Pharisees didn't. The Sadducees didn't. Some of the people in the crowd didn't. God Himself was right in their midst and they didn't even recognize Him. It was plain enough that a blind man could see it, but they missed it.

There are a lot of people like that today. Television, movies, and the ways of this world have so desensitized them to spiritual things that they can't hear or see God anywhere. Although He's right there with them in the midst of their circumstances, eager to help and eager to bless, they don't recognize Him. They think He doesn't see. They think He doesn't care. They think He has forgotten about them. They may even think He has abandoned them. They're right where the devil wants them.

But Bartimaeus didn't fall for those lies and neither should we. He knew that God, under the Old Covenant, had promised not to forsake His people.

DEUTERONOMY 31:6, 8 (AMP)

6 *Be strong, courageous, and firm; fear not nor be in terror before them, for it is the Lord your God Who goes with you; He will not fail you or forsake you.*

8 *It is the Lord Who goes before you; He will [march] with you; He will not fail you or let you go or forsake you; [let there be no cowardice or flinching, but] fear not, neither become broken*

[in spirit–depressed, dismayed, and unnerved with alarm].

Today, we can also see that God, under the New Covenant, has promised not to forsake His people.

HEBREWS 13:5 (AMP)

5 . . . *for He [God] Himself has said, I will not in any way fail you nor give you up nor leave you without support. [I will] not, [I will] not, [I will] not in any degree leave you helpless nor forsake nor let [you] down (relax My hold on you)! [Assuredly not!]*

Wow! What a promise! Kind of takes the worry out of dealing with life, doesn't it? God is in our midst! He's right here with us. He loves us. He wants to help us. We just have to recognize His presence.

Let's go back to Mark 10:47 again. It says that when Bartimaeus recognized that he was in the presence of Jesus, he began to cry out to Him. To Him. To Jesus. To the One Who has the answer to every need. Not to his mom. Not to his friends. Not to everybody else in the crowd. He cried out to Jesus. Bartimaeus knew Who to go to when he needed help.

Verse 48

> *And many charged him that he should hold his peace: but he cried the more a great deal, Thou son of David, have mercy on me.*

We see here that when the other people in the crowd heard Bartimaeus calling out to God, they told him to be quiet. Has that ever happened to you? Has anybody ever tried to discourage you from calling out to God in your time of need? Has "the crowd" ever tried to talk you out of your miracle? Or maybe it wasn't another person. Maybe it was the devil. Maybe he's tried to tell you that you're wasting your time, that God doesn't do miracles today, and that even if God *did* do miracles today, He certainly wouldn't do one for somebody like *you*!

Bartimaeus had the right idea about dealing with those kinds of people: Ignore them. And not only ignore them, but cry out all the more!

Notice that when people tried to keep him from getting what he needed from God, Bartimaeus simply "cried the more a great deal." He wouldn't let anyone or anything intimidate him. He needed something from God and he determined that nothing was going to stand in his way of getting it. Circumstances weren't going to stop him. People weren't going to stop him. Nothing was going to stop him. His mind was made up.

The word *cried* in verse 28 is the same word used in verse 27, and it doesn't mean "to sob and boo hoo." That's what a lot of people do when they run into difficulties, but that's not what Bartimaeus did. His was a different kind of cry.

The word *cry* here literally means "to call aloud" or "to scream." In other words, Bartimaeus was intense! He was calling out to God with everything in him and he wasn't about to be silenced. He knew His answer was waiting for him!

The only shout that stops God in His tracks and brings immediate results is the shout of faith.

Intensity alone, however, isn't enough. There was something special about the shout of Bartimaeus. His shout was intense, but it was also a shout of faith. (He was a believer, remember?) When he cried out to God, he cried out in faith.

A lot of times, people have something else in their shout when they cry out to God. Self-pity. Anger. Bitterness. They're either blaming God for their problems or they're blaming other people. And although those shouts may be intense, they're not going to get the desired results. Those kinds of shouts never capture the attention of God.

The only shout that stops God in His tracks and brings immediate results is the shout of faith. That's what makes your shout significant. That's what makes your shout stand out above the roar of the crowd.

Verse 48 says that Bartimaeus "cried the more a great deal." What you do in the midst of your circumstances today matters "a great deal." It's a big deal how you respond to the pressure the devil will try to put on you. It's a big deal how you respond to the people who will try to talk you out of God's plan for your life. You can't afford to let your circumstances steal your shout. You can't afford to let yourself be silenced. You've got to cry out the more in an intense shout of faith. Your answer is waiting for you!

Verse 49

And Jesus stood still, and commanded him to be called. And they call the blind man, saying unto him, Be of good comfort, rise; he calleth thee.

Once the faith of Bartimaeus arrests the attention of Jesus, Jesus commands that Bartimaeus be called to Him. The crowd follows His instructions and says to

Bartimaeus, "Be of good comfort, rise; he calleth thee." The NIV translates that "Cheer up! On your feet!" I'm sure that *did* cheer Bartimaeus up! He knew he was about to have a personal encounter with Jesus!

Allow me to make a little play on words here. Once we know we've been called by God, we'll cheer up and get going. We won't sit around begging and whining and feeling sorry for ourself, complaining that life is passing us by. We'll cheer up because we know that God loves us. We'll cheer up because we know that He has a plan for our life. We'll cheer up because we know that He will lead us into victory.

We've got to know we've been called by God. That's what makes it possible for us to serve Him without wavering. That's what gives us staying power, praying power, and finishing power. That's what makes us cheer up, no matter our situation: our call from God.

Verse 50

And he, casting away his garment, rose, and came to Jesus.

In this verse, Bartimaeus does something very significant: he throws off his garment. Why is that important? It indicates that Bartimaeus was expecting things to change once he came to Jesus.

Back in those days, people who were blind wore a special kind of robe to identify themselves. That way, anyone could tell from a distance when they were approaching a blind person.

This robe also served as an aid in receiving alms from passersby. Once the blind person sat down at his chosen location, he would form a sort of pouch in his lap with his robe so that people could toss money there as they walked by.

But what happened when Bartimaeus decided to go to Jesus? He threw that robe aside. And when he did that, I imagine the alms in his lap probably went flying as well. But Bartimaeus didn't care. He wasn't planning on needing either the robe or the alms anymore. He'd had enough of that life.

We're going to have to be aggressive with our faith.

In *The Living Bible*, verse 50 reads, "Bartimaeus yanked off his old coat and flung it aside, jumped up and came to Jesus." Sounds like he meant business, doesn't it? He was saying, "I'm not going to be blind anymore. I'm not going to be broke anymore. I refuse to settle for the kind of life I've been living. I've had enough! I know God has something better for me! I'm moving on!"

Until we've had enough of the devil's lies and his stealing from us, we'll continue to stay right where we are on the roadside of life. If we want to move on, if we want to start experiencing God's best, we're going to have to follow the example of Bartimaeus. We're going to have to mean business. We're going to have to be aggressive with our faith. We're going to have to get up, throw down all the distractions the devil's been trying to weigh us down with, and pursue the promises of God with everything that's in us. Once we do that, our victory is just around the corner.

Verse 51

> *And Jesus answered and said unto him, What wilt thou that I should do unto thee? The blind man said unto him, Lord, that I might receive my sight.*

On the surface, that sounds like a pretty dumb question, doesn't it? What did Jesus think a blind man would want from Him? The answer should have been obvious.

It *was* obvious–to Jesus. Jesus had great expectations for Bartimaeus. But Jesus can only meet us at the level of *our* expectation. Jesus could only do for Bartimaeus what Bartimaeus *believed* He could do for him. Bartimaeus had to state where *his* faith was.

Our words locate our faith. That's why Jesus asked Bartimaeus that question. Jesus already knew where *His* faith was. Now He needed to know where the faith of Bartimaeus was. It was time for Bartimaeus to say something.

If we want to start seeing God's best in our life, then it's time for us to say something. It's time to start boldly declaring our faith. It's time to start boldly decreeing the promises of God over our life. Even when our circumstances may seem to be exactly the opposite of what God has promised, we need to say what we're *expecting*, not what we're experiencing. We need to declare to God—and the devil—that we're taking our stand with God and His Word, and we're not settling for anything less!

Our words locate our faith.

Verse 52

And Jesus said unto him, Go thy way; thy faith hath made thee whole. And immediately he received his sight, and followed Jesus in the way.

Whose faith made Bartimaeus whole? The faith of Jesus? No. The faith of Bartimaeus. His *own* faith enabled him to tap into the power of God and receive what he needed–immediately.

Our deliverance is not entirely up to God. *We* have a part to play. God is ready, willing, and able to help us. He has all the power we need. He has all the wisdom we need. He has all the health we need. He has all the finances we need. He's just waiting for us.

Our deliverance is not entirely up to God.

That's exactly opposite of what most people think. They think they're waiting for God. But the truth is, God's waiting for them. He's waiting for them to trust Him. He's waiting for them to stand on His promises. He's waiting for them to quit complaining about what they're experiencing and to start declaring what they're expecting. He's waiting.

Once Bartimaeus did his part, he got results–immediately. When he moved, God was able to move. That's how it works.

Notice something else here. It says that when Bartimaeus received his sight, he "followed Jesus in the way." This wasn't just a one-time event for Bartimaeus. He wasn't there just to grab the goodies and run. If he had done that, it probably wouldn't have been long before he would have been back in similar circumstances again. No, this was the beginning of a brand new way of life for Bartimaeus. A life of believing God and standing on His Word every step of the way.

Bartimaeus had no intention of going back to the way things used to be. He had no intention of going back to begging on the side of the road. He had made up his mind that he was going to live life God's way.

We can live life God's way, too. But we'll never do it if our faith is just an event. It has to be a lifestyle. We have to follow God *in* the way, *all* the way.

CHAPTER 2

Faith In His Mercy

Faith comes in different packages. Great faith, little faith, no faith, weak faith, strong faith. The Bible talks about all of these. But right now we're concentrating on the faith of Bartimaeus, faith that got immediate results.

We can locate the faith of Bartimaeus by looking at what he asked of Jesus. He didn't ask for money. He didn't ask for sympathy. He didn't ask for power. He asked for mercy.

That's important. You see, a lot of people believe that God *can* do miracles. They're just not sure that God *will*. Believing God *can* is faith in His power. Believing God *will* is faith in His mercy. Faith in His mercy is what brings His power out of the Someday Zone and into the now. Faith in His mercy is what gets immediate results.

Believing God will is faith in His mercy.

Many people have faith in God's power, but very few have faith in His mercy. That's even true in most churches. Precious people who are born again and love God go through their entire lives uncertain as to whether or not their Heavenly Father is willing to move on their behalf. Preachers stand in their pulpits and tell their congregations that God *can* do anything for them, but then they undermine the faith of their people by telling them that they can't be sure that God *will* do anything for them.

We could probably poll our country with the following questions and predict the answers with a great degree of accuracy. Do you believe God *can* do anything? Yes. Do you believe God *can* heal? Yes. Do you believe God *can* restore marriages? Yes. Do you believe God *can* bring rebellious teens back home? Yes. Do you believe God *can* free people from drug and alcohol addiction? Yes. Do you believe God *will* do those things in *your* life or in the lives of your family members? Don't know.

They know that God *can*. They just don't know if He *will*. And until they believe that He *will*, they won't be able to release their faith to receive anything from Him.

The Nature of Mercy

Bartimaeus had faith in God's power–He knew that God *could* help him. But he also had faith in

God's mercy–He knew that God *would* help him. And that's what brought him immediate results.

What is the mercy of God? The Bible defines it in a number of different ways: grace, loving-kindness, compassion. We could say, then, that when we tap into the mercy of God, we're tapping into His grace. We're tapping into His loving-kindness. We're tapping into His compassion. That's what releases His power.

We see an example of the mercy, or compassion, of God in action in Matthew 9.

MATTHEW 9:35-36

35 *And Jesus went about all the cities and villages, teaching in their synagogues, and preaching the gospel of the kingdom, and healing every sickness and every disease among the people.*

36 *But when he saw the multitudes, he was moved with compassion on them, because they fainted, and were scattered abroad, as sheep having no shepherd.*

Compassion is what moves God. Compassion is what releases His power to operate in our lives. When we tap into His compassion, we tap into His power.

If we back up a few verses in this chapter, we discover a little more about the mercy, or compassion, of God.

MATTHEW 9:10-13

10 *And it came to pass, as Jesus sat at meat in the house, behold, many publicans and sinners came and sat down with him and his disciples.*

11 *And when the Pharisees saw it, they said unto his disciples, Why eateth your Master with publicans and sinners?*

12 *But when Jesus heard that, he said unto them, They that be whole need not a physician, but they that are sick.*

13 *But go ye and learn what that meaneth, I will have mercy, and not sacrifice: for I am not come to call the righteous, but sinners to repentance.*

Jesus was trying to help the Pharisees understand that compassion, not sacrifice, moves the heart of God, but they didn't catch what He was saying. Their minds were already made up.

You see, the Pharisees were big on sacrifice. They prayed more than anyone else. They fasted more than anyone else. They gave more money than anyone else. They even included a few good works now and then. If anyone was entitled to be blessed, they were. At least that's how they saw it.

Jesus made it plain, however, that God sees things a little differently. We don't come to God on the basis of *our* sacrifice. We come to God on the basis of *His* sacrifice. God *does* reward us for the sacrifices we make (when they're done out of a right heart), but *only* the blood of Jesus is sufficient to wipe away our sin and restore us to fellowship with God. It is *that* sacrifice, birthed out of the compassion of God, that gives us access to Him and opens the door for Him to move in our life.

Consider this example. Let's say I need something from God and I come to Him in this way: "God, I've worked hard for You all week. I've been to church three times. I've prayed and fasted. I've paid my tithe. I've given an offering. I even showed up at choir practice. Now I want You to do something for me!" Am I coming to Him based on faith in His mercy? No. I'm coming to Him based on faith in my sacrifices.

We come to God on the basis of His sacrifice.

But what if I approach Him in a different way? "Father, I love You so much. I've enjoyed worshipping You and serving You this week. It's such an honor and a privilege for me to be called Your child and to be used by You to further Your kingdom. Father, I come to You now, not on the basis of my own works but because of what You have done for me. Out of Your great love, You've made available to me everything I need in this life. And Father, I know that if

You didn't withhold Your own Son from me, You won't withhold anything else I need, either. I believe in Your mercy and Your willingness to bless me." Now I'm coming to Him based on faith in His mercy. Now I'm positioned to get immediate results.

Our sacrifices don't open the door to God's heart. Faith in His mercy opens the door to His heart. We don't come to Him based on what *we* have done. We come to Him based on what *He* has done. We have to come believing in His love and His willingness to bless us.

If we go back to Matthew 9:13 and look at it in *The Amplified Bible*, we can see this stated very plainly for us.

MATTHEW 9:13 (AMP)

13 *Go and learn what this means: I desire mercy [that is, readiness to help those in trouble]. . . .*

Notice how this verse defines mercy: readiness to help those in trouble.

The Amplified Bible is about as close as you can get to the Greek New Testament. Several years ago, a dear minister friend gave me a book of word studies out of the Greek New Testament. According to the Greek text, mercy is God's compassion, manifested in His readiness and willingness to give to us in our time of need. That's what we just read, isn't it?

That's what we have to believe about God, that He's ready and willing to help us when we're in trouble. Not just sometimes. Not just on Sundays. Always. Anytime. Anywhere. That's His nature.

Not Someday . . . Now!

Let's go back to the story of Bartimaeus and look at one more important aspect of this picture.

MARK 10:47 (AMP)

47 *And when he heard that it was Jesus of Nazareth, he began to shout, saying, Jesus, Son of David, have pity and mercy on me [now]!*

Bartimaeus believed that God *could* and He believed that God *would*. He had faith in God's power and He had faith in God's mercy. He had faith in God's readiness and willingness to move on his behalf. But he also had faith that God would demonstrate that readiness and willingness *now*. And you know what? Bartimaeus was right.

If we want to have the kind of faith that gets immediate results, then we have to step out of the

Someday Zone into the realm of the now. We have to believe that God is ready and willing to deliver us out of our trouble *now*. We have to believe that God is ready and willing to move in our life *now*. Not tomorrow. Not next week. Not someday. Now!

Too bold, you say? Not really. I didn't just make that up. It's right there in the Bible. That's what God says about Himself. All we have to do is believe it.

Have you ever watched a track meet? When it's time for each race to begin, what does the official tell the runners? "On your marks . . . get set . . . go!" Sometimes we say it this way: "Ready . . . set . . . go!" When those runners line up, take their marks, and set themselves, they are poised for action. Everything in them is ready to take off. They're just waiting for the OK. They're just waiting for permission to go.

God's mercy opens the door to everything we need from Him.

That's how we need to picture God. He's on the mark. He's set. He's ready and willing to help us. He's just waiting for us to say, "Go!" He's waiting for us to release our faith and allow Him do what He's already desiring to do in our life. He's waiting for us to say, "God, I believe you *can* do it. I believe you *will* do it. I believe you *can* and *will* do it for *me* now!"

Hebrews 4 tells us a little more about the mercy of God.

> HEBREWS 4:16 (AMP)
> [16] *Let us then fearlessly and confidently and boldly draw near to the throne of grace (the throne of God's unmerited favor to us sinners), that we may receive mercy [for our failures] and find grace to help in good time for every need [appropriate help and well-timed help, coming just when we need it].*

God's mercy opens the door to everything we need from Him. It's because of His mercy–His readiness and willingness to move on our behalf–that we can come boldly to Him when we need help and get just what we need, just when we need it. Not next week. Not next year. Not someday. Now!

God Wants To

If we never grasp anything else about God, we *must* become convinced of this: He *loves* us. Completely. Immensely. Incredibly. More than we will ever comprehend with our natural mind.

One of the best known and most widely quoted Bible passages is John 3:16–17, which talks about God's love for us. Notice how beautifully *The Amplified Bible* expounds on it.

> JOHN 3:16–17 (AMP)
> 16 *For God so greatly loved and dearly prized the world that He [even] gave up His only begotten (unique) Son, so that whoever believes in (trusts in, clings to, relies on) Him shall not perish (come to destruction, be lost) but have eternal (everlasting) life.*
> 17 *For God did not send the Son into the world in order to judge (to reject, to condemn, to pass sentence on) the world, but that the world might find salvation and be made safe and sound through Him.*

What incredible revelation about the heart of God! This is the ultimate picture of His mercy in action.

Most people grow up believing that God is mad at them, that He's out to get them, that He's out to punish them. The Word of God clearly shows us that nothing could be further from the truth. God is *for* us. He *loves* us. He *wants* to bless us. We have to believe that.

Let's switch for a moment to the story of the leper in Matthew 8. This story is loaded with insight into the heart of God.

MATTHEW 8:1-3

1 *When he was come down from the mountain, great multitudes followed him.*

2 *And, behold, there came a leper and worshipped him, saying, Lord, if thou wilt, thou canst make me clean.*

3 *And Jesus put forth his hand, and touched him, saying, I will; be thou clean. And immediately his leprosy was cleansed.*

A closer look at this story will show us why it is so important for us to believe that God loves us.

Notice that the man who comes to Jesus in this story is a leper. Lepers were outcasts from society. They were considered unclean and the rest of the people were supposed to avoid them. In fact, a leper was required to call out "Unclean! Unclean!" when people approached him so that those people would not contaminate themselves by coming into contact with the leper. To add to this shame and humiliation, most people believed that leprosy was a form of punishment from God. And to top it all off, leprosy was incurable. It was a pretty hopeless existence.

But into the apparently hopeless existence of this particular leper steps Jesus and, suddenly, everything changes. The first thing we notice is that the leper worships Jesus and acknowedges Him as Lord. That's the point where all of us need to begin if we expect to receive anything from God.

Next, the leper brings up the very issue we've been talking about in this chapter. He says, "Lord, if thou wilt, thou canst make me clean." That's King James English. Paraphrased in today's language, he said, "Lord, I know You *can* heal me. I'm just not sure You *will* heal me. I know You've got the ability. I'm just not sure You want to."

This is such an important point! Why? Because we can only exercise our faith for those things which we *know* are the will of God for us.

This leper couldn't exercise faith for his healing as long as he believed that God was using that leprosy to punish him. He had to know that God not only *could* heal him, but that God *would* heal him before he could release his faith.

We can only exercise our faith for those things which we know are the will of God for us.

Today, we're in the same position as the leper. If we believe our sickness is a punishment from God, we won't be able to exercise our faith for healing. If we believe our difficult circumstances are a punishment from God, we won't be able to exercise our faith for God to deliver us. We can't really believe Him for anything at all until we become convinced that He loves us and is ready and willing to help us *now*. We have to know that He's in our corner.

Jesus settles that question for everyone once and for all in verse 3. First, He reaches out and touches the leper. Can you imagine how that must have made the man feel? It had probably been years since anyone had touched him. He was unclean, remember? People were supposed to avoid him. But even though he may have been an outcast and a nobody to the world, the touch of Jesus told him that he was *somebody* to God.

We have to know that He's in our corner.

Then Jesus spoke and removed all doubt from the leper's mind and heart. Jesus said, "I will." The J.B. Phillips translation reads, "Of course I want to." Kenneth Wuest, a noted Greek scholar, translates it, "I am desiring it from all My heart." Any way you look at it, Jesus was saying, "I love you. I'm *for* you. I'm ready and willing to meet your need–*now*!"

That's all the leper needed to hear. *Immediately* his leprosy was cleansed. He already knew that God *could*. He just needed to know that God *would*. Once he knew that, he released his faith and got immediate results, just like Bartimaeus. It was more than faith in God's power that did it. It was faith in His mercy.

How much more clearly can God say it? If we could just master this simple but profound principle, I believe we would eliminate most of the problems we experience in receiving from God.

It's not enough for us to know *about* the love of God. We have to *believe* that He is ready and willing to manifest that love to *us* on a personal, daily basis.

> I JOHN 4:16
> 16 *And we have known and believed the love that God hath to us. . . .*

Notice what it says there. It says we have to know *and* believe God's love. Head knowledge alone won't do it. We have to *believe* it in our heart.

Don't let the truths of this story escape you. God wants you to get the message, loud and clear. He loves you! He's *for* you! Of course He wants to heal you! Of course He wants to deliver you! Of course He wants your marriage to be strong and happy! Of course He wants your children to grow up to serve Him! Of course He wants to deliver you from poverty! Of course He wants you to be blessed! He's desiring it from all His heart.

CHAPTER 3

On The Road Again

Remember where Bartimaeus was when we first saw him? Blind and begging, sitting on the side of the road. Things didn't look very good for him at that point. But then he had an encounter with Jesus that changed everything.

By the end of the story, we see Bartimaeus on the road again. He's back in the saddle. He has direction. He has purpose. He has a life to live. He's moving. He's making progress. He's going somewhere.

What about you? Are you sitting on the side of the road today instead of moving along and making progress? Have the pressures of life overwhelmed you and taken you out of the game? Are you confused and frustrated, not sure what you're supposed to do and where you're supposed to go and how you're supposed to get there?

If so, take heart. I've got good news for you. The story of Bartimaeus wasn't just a one-time event. It's a picture of what God is ready and willing to do in *your* life. You don't have to remain sidelined by the circumstances of life. You don't have to be defeated by the problems the devil dumps on your doorstep. You can get back on the road again–today!

God is not a respecter of persons. He didn't just happen to like Bartimaeus better than everybody else. He responded to the *faith* of Bartimaeus. And He'll respond to *our* faith if we exercise the same kind of faith that Bartimaeus did.

What kind of faith did Bartimaeus have? Faith in God's mercy. He knew that God *could*, but he also knew that God *would*. And he knew that God *would* for *him*.

That kind of faith brought Bartimaeus immediate results. That kind of faith will bring us immediate results, too.

Do you need some immediate results in your life today? in your marriage? in your finances? in your health? If so, then what you need is faith in God's mercy. You need to believe the love that He has for you. You need to believe in His readiness and willingness to move in your life *now*.

Tapping Into God's Mercy

How do we do that? How do we tap into the mercy of God? How do we change the way we've been believing? The Word of God gives us some ideas.

Let's look at a couple of passages, beginning with Psalm 103.

PSALM 103:17-18 (AMP)

17 *But the mercy and lovingkindness of the Lord are from everlasting to everlasting upon those who reverently fear Him, and His righteousness is to children's children–*

18 *To such as keep His covenant [hearing, receiving, loving, and obeying it] and to those who [earnestly] remember His commandments to do them [imprinting them on their hearts].*

There are several things in these verses that I believe will help us. We'll look at them one at a time.

The first thing we see is that God demonstrates His mercy to those who worship Him. Praise and worship involve expressing our love and appreciation to God for Who He is and what He has done. It blesses Him when we give Him the attention and gratitude which are rightfully His.

God wants us to worship Him privately, but there are times when we gather to worship Him publicly as well. One of those times is at church.

Actually, our public worship ought to simply be a continuation of our private worship. God doesn't live at the church. He lives in our heart. He wants us to worship Him and fellowship with Him continually throughout the day, no matter where we are. So the choir shouldn't have to sing five or six songs to pump us up when we get to church. We ought to *arrive* pumped up and ready to go because we've been fellowshipping with God all day long!

To get the most out of public worship, we have to make sure our attention stays focused on God. We can't be worried about what everybody else is doing. We can't be straining our neck to see who is there and who isn't. We can't be looking around to see what everybody else is wearing. We can't be thinking about how Sister Sandpaper offended us last week. We can't be getting upset because Brother Bothersome is sitting in our favorite spot. We can't be wondering what we're going to eat after church. We'll never be able to enter into the presence of God that way. To fully experience the presence of God, we have to think about Him and Him alone.

Meditation is what takes us from information to revelation.

The second thing we notice from Psalm 103 is that God demonstrates His mercy to those who meditate on His Word. Meditation suggests going over and over something to make it a part of us.

Meditation is what takes us from information to revelation. It's the process by which the Word of God comes alive to us.

Why is that important? Romans 10:17 tells us that faith comes by hearing the revealed Word of God. We have to know what God has said on a particular subject before we can exercise our faith there.

So if we want more faith, we have to spend more time meditating on God's Word. We have to feed on it until it becomes revelation to us, until it's real to us, until we become absolutely convinced that it's true. That's when faith begins to rise up in our heart.

The last thing we notice in Psalm 103 is that God demonstrates His mercy to those who obey Him. A lot of times we want to blame God or somebody else for our problem when the truth is that *we're* the problem! God's trying to help us, He's trying to direct us, but we keep insisting on doing things our own way. When we do that, we cut ourself off from His mercy and His blessings.

If we want to see the mercy of God manifested in our life, we have to understand that God is not the problem. He's the Answer. Once we realize that and start cooperating with Him, we'll start seeing results.

Let's go now to II Chronicles 6 and look at another verse which talks about the mercy of God.

II Chronicles 6:14 (AMP)

[14] *. . . O Lord, God of Israel, there is no God like You in the heavens or in the earth, keeping covenant and showing mercy and loving-kindness to Your servants who walk before You with all their hearts.*

This passage gives us two more keys to tapping into God's mercy: (1) serving God, and (2) being totally sold out to Him. When we make God our highest priority, we'll begin to see things happen in our life that we've never seen before. When we put Him first, everything else we need to carry on life successfully will be added to us (Matthew 6:33).

So let's recap. What are some of the ways that we can begin to tap into God's mercy?

- Worship Him.
- Meditate on His Word.
- Obey Him.
- Serve Him.
- Be totally sold out to Him.

The more we practice these principles, the more we'll tap into God's mercy. And the more we tap into His mercy, the more we'll start to see immediate results when we're in need.

The Honorable Thing

Religion tries to tell us that the honorable thing is to suffer in silence when we have needs and problems. Those things are simply our assigned lot in life–our cross–and we should bear them quietly and patiently, without expecting any help from God.

Fortunately, that's not how God sees it. As far as God is concerned, the honorable thing is to believe He is Who He reveals Himself to be in His Word: our Savior, our Deliverer, our Helper, our Counselor, our Refuge, our Strength, our Healer, our All in All. The honorable thing is to believe His promises and act on them. The honorable thing is to refuse to let the devil keep us in bondage when God has set us free. That's the honorable thing.

The more we tap into His mercy, the more we'll start to see immediate results when we're in need.

Bartimaeus did the honorable thing. (Interestingly enough, the very name *Bartimaeus* means "honorable.") He didn't let the crowd stop him from calling out to God. He didn't let his circumstances stop him. He didn't let his feelings stop him. He didn't let his past stop him. He did the honorable thing. He exercised faith in God's mercy.

God wants you to do the same. Don't give up on your marriage. Don't give up on your healing. Don't give up on your kids. Don't give up on your job. God's in your corner. It's too soon to quit!

It doesn't matter if you feel like an outcast from society (like the leper we read about in Matthew 8). It doesn't matter if nobody else seems to care about you. God cares–and He's all you need.

If you're in need of some immediate results in your life, do the honorable thing. Have faith in God's mercy. Believe that He *can* and He *will* turn things around for you.

One thing I can promise you. Once you start moving in that direction, the devil will try everything he can to get you to quit. He'll remind you of every time you ever attempted to believe God and things didn't work out. He'll remind you of every person in the church who has ever offended you. He'll try to make you mad at God, mad at your family, mad at your friends, mad at the pastor, mad at everybody. Anything to make you lose your focus. Anything to distract you from going to God and getting your needs met. Anything to keep you on the sidelines.

Let me give you a simple word of advice: Forget about all that stuff. Stop living in the past and start looking toward the future.

When Bartimaeus decided to go for God's best in his life, he threw down his robe and didn't look back. He left his alms and didn't look back. He walked away from everything that identified him as a loser. He discarded his past so that he could walk into his present and his future. He let go of everything *he* had so that he could receive everything that *God* had.

Don't let a someday mentality rob you of God's blessings today.

What's holding you back from receiving what God has for you today? What do you need to throw off so that you can step into the present and future He has planned for you? Anger? Self-pity? Excuses? Past mistakes? Offenses? Misunderstandings? Don't let those things hold you back. Throw them off. Leave them behind. They'll chain you to the past.

Bartimaeus saw himself healed, free, delivered, and on the road again. Start seeing yourself the same way.

Believe the love that God has for you. Believe that He's ready and willing to move in your life. Not next week. Not next year. Not someday. Now!

Start seeing yourself healed *now*. Start seeing yourself free *now*. Start seeing yourself delivered *now*. Start seeing yourself on the road again *now*.

Don't let a someday mentality rob you of God's blessings today. He's a right-now God and He wants to bless you right now.

Don't stop at believing that God *can* meet your need. Believe that He *will* and that He *will* do it *today*. That's right-now faith–the kind of faith that gets immediate results.

Additional copies of

Right-Now Faith

are available at fine bookstores everywhere
or directly from:

Church On The Rock
P.O. Box 1668
St. Peters, MO 63376-8668
(314) 240-7775
www.cotr.org

About The Author

Pastor David Blunt and his wife, Kim, are the pastors of Church On The Rock in St. Peters, Missouri. From the days of its small beginning of only 35 people back in 1983, God has had His hand on this ministry. Today, Church On The Rock is a dynamic, growing church of over 4,000 members, with a vision to impact its city and the world with the Gospel of Jesus Christ. This ministry is literally touching the lives of millions of people through the Internet and through the church's weekly national television broadcast, *Principles For Life*.

Pastor Blunt's insights into the Word challenge and inspire believers to grow to new levels in their relationship with God and their service to others. His practical, personable style of teaching causes the Word to come alive in the hearts of people and draws them into a personal encounter with Jesus. This life-changing ministry is committed to raising up and equipping believers to answer the call of God on their lives and to become all that He created them to be.

Also available from David Blunt are the following books:

The Incredible Benefits of Knowing God
God's Benefit: Healing
Wisdom's Winning Ways
The Power of Expectation
The Characteristics of a Plodder
This Life's for You!
How to Get Answers From God

Also available from David Blunt are the following inspirational tape series:

Authority of the Believer
The Key to Triumphant Living
Take the Limits Off of Your Life

Please send all prayer requests and inquiries to:

Pastor David M. Blunt
Church On The Rock
P.O. Box 1668
St. Peters, MO 63376-8668